STRONG ROOTS

FOSTERING GROWTH, SPIRITUALITY, AND TENACITY IN GOD'S POWERFUL SONS

BOBI GENTRY GOODWIN

Published by BGG Publications

PRINT: 979-8-9879908-3-4

EBOOK: 979-8-9879908-2-7

San Francisco Bay Area, California

Visit Bobi Gentry Goodwin online to learn more at bobigentrygoodwin.com.

Printed in the United States of America

TABLE OF CONTENTS

STRONG ROOTS BIBLE STUDY LESSONS

Dedication

To all who have struggled to find the Way.

Introduction

So then, just as you received Christ Jesus as Lord, continue to live your lives in him, rooted and built up in him, strengthened in the faith as you were taught, and overflowing with thankfulness. – Colossians 2:6-7

The *Strong Roots Small Group Curriculum* was birthed out of the desire to start a small in-home Bible study group for my daughter and her friends. The curriculum is designed to incorporate fun, food, laughter, and biblical instruction to create a memorable experience that helps both participants and leaders better understand their place in God's heart through the Bible's most beloved personalities.

Each lesson is focused on content awareness and fun activities that reinforce thematic and biblical instruction. The curriculum is set over one year with a lesson plan for each month. The lessons can also be used to conduct a twelve-week study.

My daughter, her friends, and my co-facilitators all had a blast engaging in lessons within our small group of middle school students, so I wanted to share the information with Bible-believing leaders who desire to foster growth, spirituality, and tenacity in God's powerful sons.

All lessons include:

- Group Structure

- Quarterly Theme

- Lesson Topic

- Bible Personality

- Quarterly Memory Scripture

- Group Game Activity

- Musical Playlist

The Strong Roots Bible study leader's guide is arranged in three main sections. First, we'll outline the Bible study environment and overall group meeting agenda to help you create a comfortable, structured, fun learning environment for the boys.

Then, we'll discuss the structure and key elements of the curriculum used to engage participants with the content of each lesson. Last, we'll go through the details of each lesson.

I pray the Strong Roots Bible study will help both leaders and young boys learn more about themselves, each other, and who they are as sons of the Most High King.

Letter to Group Leaders and Participants

Dear Child of God:

Growing up has its perks and disadvantages. My teenage years were full of highs and lows. Middle school was a time of first experiences. In the sixth grade, I learned to iron clothes, make bubbles with my chewing gum, and pop a wheely on my bike. The seventh grade was full of adventures, including wearing my hair down, applying make-up, and growing my fingernails as long as I could. By the time I reached eighth grade I held hands with several boyfriends, watched a ton of scary movies, and had more than a few zits.

The early teenage years of my life were also peppered with challenging times. On most days, I would find myself alone with no one to talk to. I had heard about Jesus Christ, but He was just some big guy in the sky. My grandmother had taken me to church, and I just didn't get it. Sitting in some grand building while my grandmother and her friends sang songs, waved their hands, and told me to sit still was simply no fun. I couldn't wait to get out of there and get back home. I spent most of my time at home, anyway.

Home was where I was most comfortable. By the time I was twelve, I had undergone two surgeries. Most of my older siblings had left home, and my parents were arguing a lot. I was used to sitting at home alone, but I wasn't used to being lonely. When my parents argued, I did not have anyone else I felt I could trust except that big guy in the sky.

To my surprise, we had great conversations. I would tell Him how I felt and end up feeling a lot less lonely and afraid. My conversations with Jesus Christ helped me through some of the best and worst times of my life. Sure, at the time I did not know about the Apostle Paul, Abigail, or the prophet Jeremiah. I only knew that Jesus was always there for me, and that was all I needed to know.

As I grew older, I leaned on Him even more. I found comfort in Jesus when I had to take a hard test, got bullied in high school, started my first job, and moved away for college. The conversations that started years ago multiplied as my days went on. Attending church to learn more about Jesus energized my faith in Him, but it was not until I started reading the Bible that I learned just what an impact Jesus could have on my daily life.

I learned the people in the Bible were just like me. Discovering that Abraham had to move away from his family encouraged me. I learned from Jacob and Esau that fighting with my brothers is not unusual. I was also amazed that Gideon struggled with confidence, as I did.

The Bible also taught me a lot about who I was meant to be. Knowing that the Lord can give me power like Elijah, wisdom like Solomon, forgiveness like David, or influence like Paul energized me. I learned so much from reading the Bible and the people tucked within its pages that I wanted to share just a little bit of it with you, too. Because out of all that I discovered,

I am most grateful that Jesus Christ is the same as when I met Him as a tween for the very first time: Jesus Christ is love.

He loves me and He loves you too.

In Him,

Bobi

STRONG ROOTS

BIBLE STUDY
LEADER'S GUIDE

Strong Roots Meeting Environment

TEACHER TACTICS

The Strong Roots meeting environment is designed to help leaders create clear expectations and a fun learning routine for all participants.

Please open each group meeting with prayer. Group participants should be encouraged to sit in a circle to provide a supportive container where everyone can see one another. As a group leader, you will begin the discussions and then transition to facilitator and guide as you encourage the boys to participate. Strong Roots is designed for participants and leaders to learn from each other, so questions, open dialogue, curiosity, and laughter are always encouraged.

Clear expectations and mutual respect are pillars of the Strong Roots group process. It is essential to formulate rules with input and agreement by all participants. Either post the rules or provide a copy to each participant to review as a group following the opening prayer.

Cellular phones should be discouraged. It's recommended to collect cell phones from participants before group meetings begin. It may help to offer rewards or points incentives

3

in exchange for the phones. All group members' parents or caregivers should be alerted to the cell phone policy. Group leaders are also encouraged to provide their contact info to all parents or caregivers, but refrain from cell phone usage themselves.

All group members should be encouraged to speak through-out every session. During the first few sessions, guides may choose to reward participation with incentives such as candy, reward points, thank you's, fist bumps, or applause. Begin with a check-in by giving each guide and participant a few moments to share about their week. Check-in is a time to listen, reflect, so problem-solving is discouraged. Thank each participant for sharing to help foster warmth, encouragement, and ongoing dialogue.

Repetition is an integral part of the Strong Roots group study. Memory scriptures should be discussed and reviewed at each meeting. Group participants should be rewarded for memo-rization. Group leaders can also display the memory scripture during each meeting for the group to recite.

Topic and thematic reviews are also key teaching tools for participants. Leaders can promote thematic understanding and application with well-scripted life examples. The arrange-ment of the topics and themes is designed as a progression to encourage understanding and acceptance for all partici-pants. Academic and friendship environments can be difficult to manage for students, so Strong Roots group leaders must provide both educational information and a safe space for participants to learn and ask questions. Jesus is relational, so the goal of Strong Roots is to build relationships.

Students spend most of their time in social environments around dynamic personalities. Therefore, Strong Roots should be a fun experience where the Bible personalities come alive. Group leaders are encouraged to participate in Scripture reading, discussion, and Bible personality highlights. It's important to facilitate non-judgmental dialogue that explores how the character may have felt, what they may have done, and how their environment may have impacted their choices.

Strong Roots Meeting Agenda

All group meetings should keep the same structure, so participants know what to expect. Familiarity and group norms facilitate a sense of safety among group participants. Group surprises are discouraged except on review nights.

Group Introductions

All group members (including leaders) will introduce himself, including what school he attends, his grade level, and one favorite (sports team, food, video game, song, movie, etc.) for the week.

Group Rules

During the first meeting, leaders will encourage each member to contribute one rule for the group. Make sure a scribe documents the rules for review during future meetings.

Group Check-In

All members, (including leaders) will participate in a group check-in regarding his feelings and how his week has gone. Each member can rate his week using a 1-10 scale, while leaders encourage each boy to elaborate on his rating. Candy or fruit snacks can be provided as incentives. A feelings list is provided later in this curriculum.

Review Memory Scripture

A memory scripture is provided for each quarter in the "Memorizing God's Word" section of this curriculum. Group members should review the memory scripture at each meeting.

Review Topic

Leaders will review the designated topic of the evening with the group.

Theme

Group leaders will plan and implement activities, discussion, and life application examples around the quarterly theme.

Biblical Study

The heart of each lesson is the corresponding Biblical personality study. Read and review the key scripture. Themes and questions have been provided as examples of dialogue and study.

Game Activity

Each lesson includes one suggested group game activity. Other game ideas are provided in the Game Time section of this curriculum for variety or group leader variation.

Snack

Each group meeting should include a light snack or dinner for group participants.

Prayer

Each group meeting begins and ends in prayer. Group members should be encouraged to join hands in a circle and pray together as led by group leaders or volunteer group members.

Curriculum Review Nights

On curriculum review nights, group members or leaders will choose a topic that highlights a quarterly theme. Review nights can also provide an opportunity for the boys to practice leadership roles. Group participants can rotate in leadership roles and assistant positions to help plan meeting, snack, topic, or game.

Sixty-Seconds of Silence

Each lesson includes a reflection prompt. Group participants are encouraged to sit quietly for sixty sections at end of each lesson to reflect on the prompt.

Playlist

Each lesson includes a playlist. Group participants are encouraged to listen to the playlist prior to the next group meeting. Group leaders can also use playlists in the group meeting setting, during game activities, or to generate points for group members. Group members can also suggest songs to add to playlists.

Faith Walkers

The Strong Roots curriculum also contains letters of encouragement from Faith Walkers. Faith Walkers are men of faith that have walked with Jesus throughout their lives and seek to pour into the lives of young men in the community. Group leaders can read the words of encouragement from Faith Walkers after each lesson, on curriculum review nights, or during the group process. Please review the special section included for group leaders to identify Faith Walkers in the life of their students and encourage them to complete words of encouragement.

Strong Roots Bible Study Structure

TEACHER TACTICS

Now that we've discussed the environment, we'll get into the agenda and key elements of the Strong Roots Bible Study. Teaching young people about the Bible has been one of my greatest pleasures. I have enjoyed every moment and my prayer is that you will too. Please approach each lesson with joy, curiosity, and an open heart and mind. Jesus led with love, and we can too.

It is time to have some fun! The Bible is not boring. On the contrary, it is an exciting book to read and even more fascinating to study. The Bible is filled with stories of love, conflict, hope, hardship, courage, compassion, and miracles. It is a compilation of books inspired by God in which historical accounts of people, places, and personalities jump right off the page.

Group leaders are encouraged to make the Bible lessons come alive for participants by illuminating different Bible personalities and their life experiences. The people highlighted in the Word of God are just like us in many ways. They live in communities, are surrounded by culture, have jobs, love their families, and struggle with the issues of life. In His Word, God shows us that not only does He understand our joys and pains, but He loves us through them. He is and will always be for us.

In the next section, you will learn the steps for each Bible study.

Strong Roots Bible Study Agenda

Personality Introduction

Begin by introducing the Bible personality. Each lesson includes background information, ministry highlights, Bible contemporaries, and other helpful information to inspire discussion.

Scripture Reading

All group members should be supplied with Bibles if possible. Each group member should read a portion of the scripture pertaining to the lesson.

Group Review

Facilitate discussion and understanding by encouraging group members to summarize the scripture reading.

Group Discussion

Encourage and facilitate members in a lively discussion about the lesson material, including life application examples, topic ideas, and Bible personality key points. The discussion is also the time to bridge scripture with other content in the lesson, including the topic, theme, reflection prompt, and other fun activities.

Group Game

Discuss the group game activity to contextualize the lesson.

Sixty-Seconds of Silence Reflection Prompts

Review the reflection prompt at the end of the group meeting. No dialogue is solicited from group members after the prompt is provided. Take sixty-seconds of silence and stillness for each participant to reflect internally on the prompt.

LESSON PLANS

Month	Lesson	Theme	Topic	Bible Personality
January	1	Awareness	Vision	Timothy
February	2		Vices	Jacob
March	3		Review	Review
April	4	Behavior	Courage	Nicodemus
May	5		Confidence	David
June	6		Review	Review
July	7	Character	Conviction	Joshua
August	8		Gifts	Samson
September	9		Review	Review
October	10	Discipleship	Prayer	Moses
November	11		Praise/ Worship	Daniel
December	12		Review	Review

Quarterly Lesson Review

TEACHER TACTICS

The rhythm of the Strong Roots Bible study consists of two character studies, followed by a week of review. Review nights are open slots in the curriculum intended for leaders and participants to revisit the preceding lessons, underscore takeaways, and discuss life applications in their own unique way. Here are a few suggestions for how to make memories during review nights.

Lesson reviews can be a fun time for group leaders to cultivate their creativity in thematic instruction by expressing their desires and ideas for games, playlists, or instruction as they are comfortable.

Review nights can also be used for additional group times to foster incentivized games for group participants.

Plan a fun, creative party or game night for the boys. They may be allowed to invite a friend or sibling for sports nights or a holiday-theme.

Give the boys the opportunity for their creativity and flexibility to shine by allowing them to lead the group using a similar group structure. Social media applications can also be encouraged on review nights to play games or highlight lessons.

Each of the next four sections unveils a key element of the Strong Roots Bible study used to help instructors create engaging, memorable experiences for the boys: Scripture memorization, labeling emotions, game time, and praise and worship.

Memorizing God's Word

TEACHER TACTICS

Scripture memorization is an essential part of the Strong Roots curriculum, both during the group process, and for each of the boys to hold God's Word in his heart long after group meetings have concluded.

Reinforcing the importance of God's Word among group members in a fun way can promote comfort and familiarity with the Bible, and reinforce the power of Scripture.

There are many ways to encourage and help the boys memorize Scripture.

- Display Scripture during meetings.

- Pop-quiz the boys and provide an incentive or reward to encourage group participants to memorize Scriptures.

- Prepare flash cards for at-home study.

- Provide incentives for reciting Scripture, such as a treat, a prize, or points to be tallied and redeemed for prizes at the end of quarter.

- Send memory Scriptures in birthday cards or notes to

the boys, even after the group concludes.

MEMORY SCRIPTURES

Theme	Scripture
Awareness	For I know the plans I have for you, declares the LORD, plans to prosper you and not to harm you, plans to give you hope and a future (Jeremiah 29:11).
Behavior	But God demonstrates his own love for us in this: While we were still sinners, Christ died for us (Romans 5:8).
Character	I praise you because I am fearfully and wonderfully made; your works are wonderful, I know that full well (Psalms 139:14).
Discipleship	A new command I give you: Love one another. As I have loved you, so you must love one another (John 13:34).

Labeling Emotions
TEACHER TACTICS

Young people are at varying stages of identifying and using language to label and express emotions. Complex feelings can easily overwhelm a boy's ability to navigate social situations and express vulnerability, so the Strong Roots curriculum provides a space for group members to communicate their emotions in a safe, social environment.

Emotional intelligence takes practice and intentionality. Group leaders are encouraged to help participants gain social and communication skills by expressing their feelings in a non-judgmental environment that fosters the love of God while underscoring His ability to handle, accept, and illuminate all types of emotions in His Word.

FEELINGS LIST

Angry	Determined	Hurt	Regretful
Arrogant	Disappointed	Jealous	Relieved
Bashful	Disbelieving	Joyful	Sad
Beautiful	Disgusted	Lonely	Satisfied
Blissful	Embarrassed	Loved	Scared
Bored	Excited	Mad	Shocked
Brave	Exhausted	Mindful	Strong
Bullied	Frustrated	Miserable	Surprised
Calm	Goofy	Optimistic	Sympathetic
Cautious	Grieving	Passionate	Tranquil
Concerned	Guilty	Peaceful	Victimized
Confident	Happy	Pessimistic	Victorious
Confused	Hopeful	Positive	Wonderful
Curious	Humorous	Powerful	Worried

Time to Grow
TEACHER TACTICS

Studying the Word of God produces change in every believer. Students of the Bible learn about God's goodness and His righteousness. The Strong Roots curriculum encourages group leaders to highlight biblical and topical instruction through the lens of overarching themes that promote right living.

Four themes were chosen to help leaders foster growth among the boys. Group participants should leave the twelve-week study with improved skills in Awareness, Behavior, Character, and Discipleship (A, B, C, Ds). The earlier students are taught the A, B, C, Ds, the quicker they will learn and master them.

Each skill is backed by Scripture.

A= Awareness

"The wisdom of the prudent is to give thought to their ways, but the folly of fools is deception" (Proverbs 14:8).

B= Behavior

"Don't let anyone look down on you because you are young, but set an example for the believers in speech, in conduct, in love, in faith and in purity" (1 Timothy 4:12).

C= Character

"Not only so, but we also glory in our sufferings, because we know that suffering produces perseverance; perseverance, character; and character, hope. And hope does not put us to shame, because God's love has been poured out into our hearts through the Holy Spirit, who has been given to us" (Romans 5:3-5).

D= Discipleship

"By this everyone will know that you are my disciples, if you love one another"(John 13:35).

Game Time
Teacher Tactics

Group games should be a time of excitement. Instead of teaching, Strong Roots group leaders can take a back seat and watch the fun unfold. Some games require leader participation. For other games, leaders will check in with participants or simply join in the fun and banter.

Leaders will take an opportunity to link the group game to the lesson as the games wrap up. Teams are used during certain game events, but student variation amongst the teams throughout the group process is highly encouraged. Group leaders should always select teams diplomatically and in an unbiased way. Typically, games are followed by dinner or a snack.

Group Game Activities

Jesus Tag

Group members select one member of the group to play Jesus. The group member playing Jesus is given a thirty-second head start. Jesus is then hunted by the rest of the group. The game is designed to open up a discussion about how Jesus was sought out before His capture and killing on the cross.

Jellybeans

Group leaders provide any type of mixed jellybeans. Assorted flavored jellybeans work best. Group leaders mix up jellybeans and allow boys to grab the same number of jellybeans that are in the group. The boys eat and describe what the jellybean looked like and if the taste matched their vision of the bean. This activity can also be done with baby food where the boys blind-taste and guess the food. Group leaders lead a discussion about never judging a book by its cover.

Famous Personalities

Tape a cutout of a celebrity on each boy's back. Popular personalities for boys at the current time work great, but group leaders can also mix in Bible personalities. Each boy must ask questions until the boy wearing the personality figures out which celebrity photo is taped to his back. Group leaders can lead group members in discussions about reputation.

Girl Crazy

Group members are to participate in a scavenger hunt to find pictures of girls and girl-related items hidden in the home, church, or yard. The group member or group team with the most items found wins a prize. This game can also be used to engage group members in a discussion about discovering things of value, dealing with distraction, and the biblical personality of Samson.

Charades
Traditional Game

Group leaders can lead a discussion with group members about the power of silence and using your words constructively.

Egg Toss
Traditional Game

Group leaders can engage group members in a discussion about being tossed about in the world and the fragility of life. Discussions can also center around how persevering through tough things can make a person stronger. Some eggs can be boiled or leaders can use candy-filled eggs with some sealed shut to highlight an example of the sealing of the Holy Spirit.

Wake Up

Separate the boys into multiple teams. Each group participant from the opposite team takes a turn laying down. The other group team members surround him and take turns trying to make the boys laugh. The team that wakes up the most participants win. This game is a great way to discuss evangelism and the impact people can have on one another.

Write a Letter to Your Future Self

Instruct the boys to write a one-page letter to their future self, ideally at age thirty. Then the boys work together along with leaders to write Jesus's letter to His 30-year-old self from the viewpoint of their current age. Group leaders can also use this time to discuss other male figures that made biblical or historical societal impacts at a young age.

S'mores

Each group participant can assemble smores in a sandwich bag for their male teachers, uncles, coaches, or leaders. Fathers should be excluded. The boys may also include a thank you note indicating that they wish there were *"S'more men of valor"* like their leaders. The game is to help boys identify other men of value in their community.

Wink Game

Leaders choose a member of the group to be "Judas." All the boys assemble in a circle. "Judas" winks unsuspectedly at their group members in the circle and "kills" them with a wink. The person who was "killed" must leave the group while the other group members guess who the "Judas" is.

Stomp the Yard

Group members should be separated into teams, blow up balloons, and place numbers in them according to colors. Each team picks a color and then outside, the boys try to smash opposing teams' balloons. Each team with the most points from the opposite teams' numbers wins. Group leaders can lead members in a discussion about the impact of stepping on others to get ahead.

Flip the Bottle Game

Each boy is provided with three water bottles. Each water bottle contains ¼, ½, and ¾ filled with liquid. Each participant flips the bottle to identify which participant's bottle can land upright the most times. Each boy gets three chances. The boy with the most upright bottles wins a prize. Group leaders can then facilitate a discussion about the filling of the Holy Spirit and the ability to walk upright when facing challenges.

Match Game

Each boy writes a positive statement about himself and other group members on sticky notes. The boys place the sticky notes all over the room, return to their seats, and then close their eyes for thirty seconds. When they open their eyes, they may be unleashed to find sticky notes that match in pairs of two. The boy with the most matching sticky notes wins. Group leaders can lead members in discussion on how much people have in common and the power of affirmation.

Leader Game

The Leader Game is good old-fashioned Simon Says with a twist: all the boys are blindfolded except the boy leading the game. This game can be used to discuss the power of faith and belief when we are not able to see things clearly.

Stay Afloat

Boys are separated into teams. Each team is provided with popsicle sticks and glue. Each team makes a boat. Boats are tested in a sink or a container filled with water to ascertain if it floats. Group leaders then identify if any boats float and start placing pennies on floating boats until they sink. Group leaders then can lead a discussion with boys about obstacles that can impact their ability to stay afloat.

Positive Affirmations/Mason Jar

Each group participant writes positive affirmations on slips of paper and fill a mason jar to the top for a special teacher, principal, or pastor. Jars can be delivered by group leaders or students.

Praise and Worship
TEACHER TACTICS

Young people enjoy listening to music. Many pop in their headphones and zone out. The Strong Roots curriculum developer built a curated playlist of worship music to help the boys both zone out and tune in to each Bible lesson.

Group leaders can play praise and worship music during their study or game times. Leaders are also encouraged to recommend group participants listen to songs from the selected playlist to help encourage them to encounter God in a different way.

Suggested Playlists

Lesson 1 Topic: Vision
Track 1: Good Good Father by Chris Tomlin
Track 2: What You're Worth by Mandisa
Track 3: Do Life Big by Jaime Grace

Lesson 2 Topic: Vices
Track 1: Good Fight by Unspoken
Track 2: Victory by Tye Tribett
Track 3: I Surrender by V. Rose

Lesson 3 Topic: Review
Track 1: Nothing Ever by Citizen Way
Track 2: God is on the Move by 7eventh Time Down
Track 3: Build my Life by Bri Babineaux

Lesson 4 Topic: Courage
Track 1: The River by Jordan Feliz
Track 2: Can't Give Up Now by Mary Mary
Track 3: I Believe it Now by Sideway Prophets & Olivia Lane

Lesson 5 Topic: Confidence
Track 1: Hello Fear by Kirk Franklin
Track 2: Nobody by Casting Crowns
Track 3: Gold by Britt Nicole

Lesson 6 Topic: Review
Track 1: Even if by MercyMe

Track 2: Overcoming by William McDowell & Martha Munizzi
Track 3: Imperfect Me by Smokie Norful

Lesson 7 Topic: Conviction
Track 1: Fear be Quiet by Hnry featuring Tedashii
Track 2: Unshakeable by Fred Hammond & United Tenors
Track 3: Broken People (feat. DOE) by Israel & New Breed

Lesson 8 Topic: Gifts
Track 1: Intentional by Travis Greene
Track 2: E6 by Evvie McKinney
Track 3: Blessings by Lecrae

Lesson 9 Topic: Review
Track 1: You Say by Lauren Daigle
Track 2: Never Lost by Tribl & Marverick City Music
Track 3: Goodness of God by CeCe Winans

Lesson 10 Topic: Prayer
Track 1: Haven't Seen it yet by Danny Gokey
Track 2: Pray by Koryn Hawthorne
Track 3: Find You on my Knees by Kari Jobe

Lesson 11 Topic: Praise
Track 1: Put a Praise on it by Tasha Cobbs Leonard (Feat. Kierra Sheard)
Track 2: I'm Yours by Casey J
Track 3: Jireh by Maverick City Music (Feat. Chandler Moore & Naomi Raine)

Lesson 12 Topic: Review
Track 1: Fix my Eyes by King & Country
Track 2: Your Great Name by Natalie Grant
Track 3: Take Me to the King by Tamela Mann

Faith Walkers

Words of Encouragement from Mr. Don
Favorite Scripture: Jeremiah 29:11

You Are Special

During your journey in life, you will have some ups and downs. There will be times when you feel happy and times when you feel sad. There will be times in your life when you hear, "Yes," but also sometimes when you will hear, "No." However, today there is something I want to tell you and something I want you to know.

You are important, beautiful, and loved. God created human beings, including you, in His image and His likeness. You are special to Him.

All boys and girls are created by God (Genesis 1:26-27). God loves you so much that He sent His one and only Son into the world so that you might live through Him (John 3:16). Listen, God is here for you. God doesn't want you to worry or fear. He's talking to you when He says, "So do not fear, for I am with you" (Isaiah 41:10 NIV).

You might not understand it all right now, but I want you to know that God has a wonderful plan for your life. "'For I know the plans I have for you,' declares the Lord, 'plans to prosper you and not to harm you, plans to give you hope and a future'" (Jeremiah 29:11 NIV).

Isn't that great news? You will prosper. You will be successful. You will be victorious. Yes, you!

Words of Encouragement from Mr. Burch
Favorite Scripture: Romans 8:28-30

Go For It

God can see your end from the beginning of time. He sees you, knows you, and has a purpose for your life. He has equipped you to be great. Hold your head up high and go through life knowing that you are an heir to the throne of God, and your best is yet to come.

God has set you up for greatness. Set goals, follow God, trust Him, and leave the rest to Him. Go to school and get a college degree. Start your own business. Reach for the sky because this world is full of opportunities. If you set your heart on Christ and ask Him for His help, He will lead, direct, and guide you. If you put God first and be led by the Spirit of the Lord, you can accomplish all the desires of your heart. Nothing is impossible with God.

Words of Encouragement from Mr. Goodwin
Favorite Scripture: 1 Corinthians 15:58

You Are a Winner

Most people that I know love to win and do not like to lose. I want you to know and understand that you are a winner. Hear me when I say that victory is yours if you put your trust in God. "Trust in the Lord with all your heart and lean not on your own understanding; in all your ways submit to Him, and He will make your paths straight" (Proverbs 3:5-6 NIV).

The apostle Paul compared our path to a faithful fight and to a race. Listen, your fight may not always be simple and your race may not always be easy, but hold on to your faith. When the battle seems rough, hold on to your faith. When the race seems tough, hold on to your faith. I want you to know that the Lord said, "For the battle is not yours but God's" (2 Chronicles 20:15b). God has your back, and He has you covered. His hands are on you! You will win!

Winners become great from practicing. Just like sports, trust and faith get stronger with practice. The way you can practice your faith is by reading the Bible. "Consequently, faith comes from hearing the message, and the message is heard through the word about Christ" (Romans 10:17 NIV).

You can also practice by praying and praising God. Praying is direct communication with God and praising is showing Him honor. Promise me you will practice. I believe you will. I want you to know your leader loves you; I love you, and God loves you even more, and with all that love, who can lose?

Words of Encouragement from Mr. Oden
Favorite Scripture: Joshua 1:8-9

Seek God's Voice

One of the most important things you can do as a young man is find out what God's plan is for your life. God created you and has a specific, desired path for you. Once you find this path and get moving on it, you will have a great sense of fulfillment, joy, and energy to push forward in life. This requires a strong, consistent prayer life so you can learn to know God's voice in your life. Don't get frustrated if you can't discern God's voice initially, because, like young Samuel in the Bible, it takes time to know that voice (1 Samuel 3:1-10). However, once you discern God's voice, you'll hear Him speaking to you like He did to Joshua (Joshua 1:2-9). God desires to lead and encourage you. If you seek God with all your heart, and His will for your life, He will make His ways known to you, and He will cause you to have great success.

Words of Encouragement from Mr. Nance
Favorite Scripture: Psalm 73:26

A Work in Progress

To the young men that bear the burden and responsibilities of this generation,

Please understand, although you may be willing to be the standard, just know there will be *sometimes* moments that all men experience. You will make wrong choices sometimes. You will follow your heart and it will lead you to heartache sometimes. And you may even fail sometimes, but always reflect on Psalm 73:26 and be encouraged. It says, "My flesh and my heart may fail, but God is the strength of my heart and my portion forever" (Psalm 73:26 NIV).

Mistakes and missteps are necessary for us to appreciate achievements. You will never appreciate victory unless you have experienced some defeat, and you will never understand success until you've had failure. But throughout it all, remember these two things: God will strengthen you and don't make your *sometimes* be all the time.

**Words of Encouragement from Mr. Sullivan
Favorite Scripture: Proverbs 3:5-6**

A Good Mentor

Every teenager should have someone to look up to. A mentor is invaluable. My mentor was my dad. I saw firsthand his love for Jesus Christ, my mother, and his children. His work ethic was unmatched in my eyes. He worked tirelessly at two full-time jobs to provide for his family. And as children, he always ensured we went to church. My dad was a busy man, but he always made time. He worked a lot and even when he was not present at church due to his work schedule, he provided us with an offering and a check for his tithes.

I also marveled at how people responded to him and how he treated others. He was such an example that it was a no-brainer for me to pattern myself after him as he followed God. He was a consistent man of God. The sound advice he afforded me as a teenager was always on point, even when I did not listen. He taught me to evaluate the consequences of my actions.

Young man, I urge you to find someone who loves Jesus Christ, is respectful of others, and is consistent to serve as a mentor for you. Look for someone who loves God, provides for his community, and is willing to make sacrifices for those he loves. Look for a man who does all this while sitting in a space of humility, without seeking attention. This man is a man of valor who can serve as a wonderful mentor for you in your walk with Jesus Christ.

Words of Encouragement from Mr. Turner
Favorite Scripture: Psalm 73:26

Know Who You Are

If a puppet master's puppet calls you out by name, with whom would you be upset, the puppet or the puppet master? Of course, you don't get upset with the puppet; the puppet master controlled it. How does that relate to today?

The devil is quite a puppet master, and he has many puppets. Instead of getting mad and upset with people, get upset with the devil and his plans and schemes. The devil's biggest fear is that we become aware of who we are in God.

Know who you are in Christ Jesus because the enemy likes to oppose your true identity. You are the very body of Christ. Whenever the enemy and the storms of life arise, you must have a firm foundation in Christ. Often, men find it difficult to find their identity because they do not know who they are in Christ.

It does not matter if people don't like you. People are not the problem; neither are they your answer. The answer is simple. You must love God, people, and yourself. It is time to change your mindset by focusing on what God has told you. The Bible says you are part of a royal family (1 Peter 2:9). If God is King and you are His child, then you are an heir to His throne (Galatians 4:6-7), no matter what or who comes against you. Stand tall in the truth of who and whose you are.

Words of Encouragement from Mr. Henry
Favorite Scripture: Psalm 139:14

Notes to a Young Me

Excuse me, young me, may I have a word with you? Listen, never allow anyone else to define who you are. You are a marvelous work of God. If you want to know who you are, simply ask your Creator. Don't allow fear (false evidence appearing real) to dictate how you navigate life. Fear is only a dark room where the enemy exposes the negatives.

Before becoming a king, David found himself in a cave, later joined by his family and many hurting folks. When he realized the leader God created him to be, David led those people, including his family, out of the cave to victory. David was not there because he had done something wrong. He was on the run because of the current king's jealousy.

Young me, do not allow other people's insecurities to put you in a dark cave. Don't allow others to define you. One day, the man in you will rise up as you face life's challenges and say, "I will bless the Lord at all times," which means you will not walk in fear. Walk as the king God created you to be. Thank you, young me, for a moment of your time.

Words of Encouragement from Mr. Isaac
Favorite Scripture: Psalm 73:26

Know God's Promises

Trust God and seek Him in everything you do. God rewards those that seek Him. Don't rely only on others. Remember, God is there for you, too. His Word is living and it can change your life for the better.

It's up to you to open your Bible and read the Word. In His Word, many promises are available for you. I've learned that the very moment I study and believe one of God's promises, He activates that promise over my life.

Young man, study the Word of God, meditate on His Word, and pray the Word to know what God has in store for you. Go to sleep and wake up with God on your mind. Get hungry and thirsty for God. You'll have more confidence.

Self-doubt can disappear when you know God, accept yourself, and believe in His promises. It's easy to stand your ground when you stand on His promises.

You can always walk in boldness and confidence with your head held high. You can no longer worry about what others think (Proverbs 29:25). You can make better decisions (James 1:5). You are redeemed and forgiven by the grace of Jesus Christ (Ephesians 1:7).

You are chosen by God, and you are holy and beloved (Colossians 3:12). Your past doesn't determine who you are. You may make a mistake, but your mistake is not who you are (Isaiah

43:25). You are more than a conqueror (Romans 8:37). You can do all things through Christ (Philippians 4:13). You have perfect peace when trouble comes (Philippians 4:7). You are blessed (Jeremiah 17:7-8). You are victorious and a winner in everything you do (Romans 8:31).

Now, do you believe in God and His Promises?

Words of Encouragement from Community Partner
Favorite Scripture:

_____

_____

_____

_____

_____

_____

_____

_____

_____

_____

_____

_____

Words of Encouragement from Community Partner
Favorite Scripture:

_____

_____

_____

_____

_____

_____

_____

_____

_____

_____

_____

_____

STRONG ROOTS

BIBLE STUDY LESSONS

Lesson 1
TIMOTHY

Bible Personality
Timothy

Scripture
Each group member should read a portion of scripture pertaining to tonight's lesson.

Topic
Vision: The act or power of seeing: Sight. [1]

Theme
Awareness

Scripture Reading
2 Timothy 1:1-14

Scripture Summary

Paul is an apostle and teacher of the Word of God, but he cannot do it alone. Throughout his journey, he encountered incredible people who helped him along the way. One of those people was Timothy.

Timothy was a young man raised to believe in Jesus Christ by his mother and grandmother. He also learned the Holy Scriptures. Paul and Timothy were more than friends or even mentor and mentee. Their bond resembled a father-son relationship, so it hurt to be separated.

Paul remembered and prayed for Timothy. As his mentor and father in the faith, Paul hoped Timothy would have a wonderful relationship with God. He wants his son Timothy to know what a treasure he is and what kind of special gifts God stored inside him. Paul didn't want him to be afraid. He wanted Timothy to be fearless in knowing that God loves him and gave him power, self-discipline, and the capacity to love.

Paul encouraged Timothy that no matter what, he should not be ashamed of himself, Paul, or God. Instead, he should live his life in holiness through God's grace for him and all people. Paul reminded Timothy to never forget what he learned and to guard it with the help of the Holy Spirit.

Key Points

Timothy was a young man who devoted his life to Christ. He was raised in a home with parents from two different cultures. His maternal relatives instructed Timothy in the Scriptures from an early age. Timothy eventually left home to travel with his mentor Paul to share the Gospel.

Possible Talking Points

- Timothy's youth

- Planning for the future

- Timothy's genuine faith

- Living in communities where cultures clash

- Taking risks

- Creating valuable relationships

- Sharing the Good News

Leader Notes

_____

_____

_____

_____

_____

_____

_____

_____

_____

_____

_____

Discussion

- Who was Timothy's friend? Are mentors and friends valuable?

- Why was this letter written to Timothy?

- What was Timothy's friend's vision for him?

- What are your friends' and family's visions for you? How would they describe you?

- What traits do you want others to know about you?

Game Suggestion

Famous Personalities

Sixty-Second
Reflection Question

Timothy left his grandmother, Lois, and mother, Eunice, to pursue the ministry of Jesus Christ. What do you have to leave behind to follow your vision?

_____

_____

_____

_____

_____

_____

_____

_____

_____

_____

_____

Lesson 2
Jacob

Bible Personality
Jacob

Scripture
Each group member reads a portion of scripture pertaining to tonight's lesson.

Topic
Vices: A habitual and usually trivial defect or shortcoming: Foible.[1]

Theme
Awareness

Scripture Reading
Genesis 25:19-27
Genesis 27:1-24

Scripture Summary

Jacob was a twin. He and his older brother, Esau, were an answered prayer to his parents. Isaac and Rebekah could not have children at first, but God answered their prayer and gave them two sons.

Jacob and Esau had many struggles with each other. Their struggles began before they were born while in their mom's stomach. The Lord told Rebekah that her sons were destined to become rivals. Each man would be the leader of a different nation, and the older brother would serve the younger.

Just as the Lord said, the brothers' struggles in the womb continued after they were born. They had difficulties living at home together, and this caused many rifts between them. To make matters worse, Jacob's mother favored him over his older brother.

The trouble continued when their father, Isaac, was old and nearly blind. Isaac wanted to give his eldest son his birthright blessing after his final meal before he died. Jacob's mother did not want her oldest son to receive the father's blessing, so she devised a scheme to trick him into blessing her favorite son, Jacob. The two were successful in their plot. After Jacob dressed up like his older brother, prepared a meal for his father, and told him he was Esau, Isaac gave him the blessing intended for Esau.

Key Points

Jacob and Esau were brothers, but they were different in many ways. Esau loved the outdoors and was a hunter and Jacob preferred to stay at home. Jacob became his mother's favorite son. He listened to her instead of honoring both his parents. He deceived and lied to his father even after being given a chance to tell the truth. He stole his brother's blessing and eventually paid a hefty price.

Possible Talking Points

- Peer pressure

- Lying

- Sibling relationships

- Favoritism

- Deception

- Challenging authority

- Standing up for what is right

Leader Notes

_____

_____

_____

_____

_____

_____

_____

_____

_____

_____

_____

_____

Discussion

- Why was receiving a blessing from his father important to Jacob?

- What could have Jacob done in this situation? What is his vice?

- How do you handle conflict?

- How did Jacob's mother encourage him to sin?

- What do you do when you feel conflicted between right and wrong?

Game Suggestion

Flip the Bottle

Sixty-Second
Reflection Question

We all make mistakes. Think about a time when someone encouraged you to do something wrong. What did you do? What could you have done differently?

_____

_____

_____

_____

_____

_____

_____

_____

_____

_____

_____

Lesson 3

REVIEW

Bible Personality
Review

Scripture
Review

Theme
Awareness

Discussion
Open

Potential Key Points
Open

Game Suggestion
Open

Sixty-Second Reflection Activity

Write the memory Scripture in your own words. What does this Scripture mean to you?

"For I know the plans I have for you," declares the Lord, "plans to prosper you and not to harm you, plans to give you hope and a future." Jeremiah 29:11

_____

_____

_____

_____

_____

_____

_____

_____

_____

_____

_____

Lesson 4

NICODEMUS

Bible Personality
Nicodemus

Scripture
Each group member reads a portion of Scripture pertaining to tonight's lesson.

Topic
Courage: Mental or moral strength to venture, persevere, and withstand danger, fear, or difficulty.[1]

Theme
Behavior

Scripture Reading
John 3:1-21

Scripture Summary

Nicodemus was a leader in his community. He was a Pharisee, part of the religious elite. Pharisees were scholars in Jesus's community, and they were sticklers about everyone following the rules and laws, even though at times they didn't follow them.

One day, Nicodemus decided to visit Jesus. He waited until it was nighttime to find Him. Then, Nicodemus posed a series of questions to Jesus and acknowledged Him as a teacher God had sent, but not as the Messiah.

Jesus took time to sit and talk with Nicodemus. He answered his questions. He informed Nicodemus that to see the kingdom of God, something very specific had to happen—he must be born again. Jesus explained that re-birth was not re-entering a mother's womb, but being reborn spiritually. He also informed him that spiritual matters like the Holy Spirit cannot be easily understood through human reasoning or rationale. Jesus likened the Holy Spirit to the wind blowing: you can hear it and see what it does, but you can't see the wind or decide which way it will go.

Jesus is a great teacher. He explained to his new student that even though Nicodemus is a teacher himself, he can't understand. He explained that if Nicodemus can't explain things that happen on earth, then how could he believe spiritual things?

Jesus reports that faith is a matter of belief, and to be born again in the Spirit, we must believe in Him as the Messiah. He further explained the love of God does not come from a place of judgment. He simply stated that God loves people so much that He sent His Son to save them.

Key Points

Nicodemus was curious. He wanted to know more about Jesus. He was not comfortable seeking Him out openly, but he still found a way to talk with Him. Nicodemus wanted his questions answered, and he was not too afraid to ask.

Jesus was kind to Nicodemus. He answered all his questions, despite Nicodemus coming to see Him late. He not only answered his questions, but he gave him new information. Jesus shared God's love for Nicodemus and explained how he could become part of the family of faith.

Possible Talking Points

- Courage

- Fear

- Power and control

- Questioning God

- Re-birth

- Taking action

- Learning God's Word

Leader Notes

_____

_____

_____

_____

_____

_____

_____

_____

_____

_____

_____

Discussion

- What do you think happened to Nicodemus after he met Jesus?

- How do you handle fear?

- What are some difficult things about listening only to authority figures?

- Describe the most courageous act you have ever seen or heard of. How did Nicodemus display courage by coming to Jesus at night?

- What is salvation?

Game Suggestion

Girl Crazy

Sixty-Second Reflection Question

Nicodemus had to face his fears to talk to Jesus. What fears do you need to face or bring to Jesus today?

_____

_____

_____

_____

_____

_____

_____

_____

_____

_____

_____

_____

Lesson 5

DAVID

Bible Personality
David

Scripture
Each group member reads a portion of scripture pertaining to tonight's lesson.

Topic
Confidence: A feeling or consciousness of one's powers or of reliance on one's circumstances. [1]

Theme
Behavior

Scripture Reading
1 Samuel 17:12-37

Scripture Summary

David was the youngest child of eight sons. His three other brothers had already joined King Saul's army to defend the nation from the Philistines. David lived at home and helped his elderly father, Jesse, with their livestock.

He frequently traveled to the battlefield to bring supplies to his brothers and the Israelite army, and to bring back a report to Jesse about his sons. Traveling back and forth from home to the battlefield couldn't be easy, but David listened to his father.

One day, during a delivery to the battlefield, David heard a commotion. A Philistine giant named Goliath was bullying the Israelite army, and they were scared. The army retreated even though the King Saul offered a handsome reward to anyone who would defeat the giant.

David could not believe these happenings. This giant was one man against the God of Israel and there was even a reward to defeat him. He had heard all that he needed to hear. He told other soldiers he would fight Goliath. David's brother overheard him and became angry, but David did not let his brother deter him. He kept on talking and was soon summoned by King Saul. The young boy had courage in the Lord, so he agreed to fight the giant. David believed and was victorious.

Key Points

As the youngest son, he was discounted by many, but David was a young man with conviction. He was a hard worker, obedient to authority, and took his responsibilities seriously. He rose to the occasion despite many challenges. He believed in his God and himself instead of what other people thought of him.

Possible Talking Points

- Self Confidence

- Leadership

- Facing Obstacles

- Taking Responsibility

- Internal strength

- Being yourself

- Faith in God

Leader Notes

Discussion

- What are the giants in today's society?

- Name a few young people that made great change.

- What gives you confidence?

- Give examples of experiences in David's life that could have made him lack confidence?

- How does the perspective of others impact your peer group? How does the perspective of others impact you?

- What is the difference between confidence and arrogance?

Game Suggestion

Write a Letter to Your Future Self

Sixty-Second Reflection Question

David had confidence. Why do you think confidence is important to help people face difficult times? Where can you use more confidence in your own life?

Lesson 6

REVIEW

Bible Personality
Review

Scripture
Review

Theme
Behavior

Potential Key Points
Open

Discussion
Open

Game Suggestion
Open

Sixty-Second
Reflection Activity

Write memory Scripture in your own words. What does this Scripture mean to you?

But God demonstrates his own love for us in this: While we were still sinners, Christ died for us.Romans 5:8

_____

_____

_____

_____

_____

_____

_____

_____

_____

_____

_____

Lesson 7

Joshua

Bible Personality
Joshua

Scripture
Each group member reads a portion of Scripture pertaining to tonight's lesson.

Topic
Conviction: A strong persuasion or belief. [1]

Theme
Character

Scripture Reading
Numbers 13:1-33
Numbers 14:1-9

Scripture Summary

The Lord had given His people instructions. He spoke to Moses, the leader of the Israelite community, and informed him to pick other leaders from the twelve tribes of Israel to go on a mission. Moses followed the Lord's instructions and chose twelve men to head into Canaan, the land the Lord promised to give them. Moses gave all the leaders clear instructions on how to carry out their mission and exactly what they were looking for.

The men followed Moses's instructions and returned to report what they had seen. They also provided extra information about the people who lived there. Many of the twelve leaders gave horrific tales about the men who lived in Canaan. The leaders felt small and insignificant when they compared themselves to the men in Canaan. Their confidence shrank, so they did not want to go back to the land and take what the Lord had given them.

Caleb was a leader in the community who challenged the other leaders' reports. He declared confidence in their ability to take the land. He even tried to quiet all the naysayers, but it didn't work. The other leaders eventually became so fearful that they cried all night and turned against both Moses and his right hand, Aaron. They even turned against the Lord and His plan for them.

Joshua and Caleb decided to address the community. They declared their faith in God and His power to give them what they needed in this situation. They encouraged the leaders not to rebel against the Lord, but to have faith in Him instead. They displayed confidence and boldness as they announced the land was wonderful, and that the Lord would bring them to it safely under His protection.

Key Points

Joshua and Caleb were leaders in the Israelite community. They went with their brethren to spy on the land God was giving them as an inheritance. Once in the land, Joshua and Caleb saw things very differently from their brothers. They saw opportunity, hope, and potential. They followed instructions and saw things from a lens of faith. These leaders then had to confront their brothers regarding their lack of faith and hope. Standing on their conviction, these men stood up in the face of peer pressure and adversity.

Possible Talking Points

- Confidence in God

- Listening to God

- Facing the crowd

- Men in leadership roles

- Importance of preparation

- Power in the tongue

- Boldness

Leader Notes

_____

_____

_____

_____

_____

_____

_____

_____

_____

_____

_____

Discussion

- How do you show confidence?

- What characteristics make a good leader?

- What does boldness mean?

- How do you tackle difficult situations, especially when other people are watching?

- What do you value in your relationships with other young men, women, and leaders?

Game Suggestion

Positive Affirmations/Mason Jar

Sixty-Second Reflection Question

Joshua and Caleb had to face a hostile crowd. They had to stick to their conviction when everyone else thought they were wrong. How did their belief in God and their strength help them? How can your belief in God and your strength help you when faced with difficulties?

Lesson 8

SAMSON

Bible Personality
Samson

Scripture
Each group member reads a portion of Scripture pertaining to tonight's lesson.

Topic
Gifts: A notable capacity, talent, or endowment. [1]

Theme
Character

Scripture Reading
Judges 14:10-18
Judges 16:4-22

Scripture Summary

Samson was a very special man. He was dedicated to God before he was born, so after his birth, God gifted him with a special ability. Samson was a Nazarite who was given incredible strength, but that gift came with rules and responsibilities that Samson sometimes forgot.

Samson was getting married, and he was ready to celebrate. Immediately after his wife's parents introduced him to some new guys, Samson threw himself right into the center of attention. He became the life of the party by offering the men a challenge to solve his riddle and make some money. The only challenge was that if they could not solve the riddle, they would lose money.

The men agreed to Samson's terms and put their heads together, but they could not solve the riddle. In frustration, the men threatened his new wife. They wanted the answer or else there would be dire consequences. Samson's wife obliged and sought an answer from her new husband. Initially, Samson wouldn't disclose the answer to the riddle, but his new wife frustrated him by asking every time they were together. After she pestered him for seven days, he gave in. Samson's wife told the men his secret, and they confronted him with the answer. Samson now had a debt to pay, which led to bloodshed, anger, and marital problems.

Samson and his wife separated. Eventually, he found his eyes settling on a new woman named Delilah. Samson fell head over heels in love with her, but she hid something from him.

Delilah kept her love of money a secret. While in a relationship with him, she participated in financial negotiations with the rulers of his enemies in a plot to harm him.

Her business partners wanted to know the secret to Samson's strength. Samson refused to tell her at first, but just like his first wife, Samson's new woman taunted him until he got frustrated and revealed his secret. Of course, Delilah used the information against him. Samson was offered into the hands of his enemies, but without the Lord's presence. He no longer had the gift of strength the Lord had provided, so he was imprisoned and tortured by his enemies.

Key Points

Samson was a chosen man of God. God had gifted him with special abilities. He knew he needed God's presence, but sometimes Samson lost his way. He struggled with setting clear boundaries and expectations for people and himself. Samson was impulsive, which led to some bad decisions.

Possible Talking Points

- Gifts and abilities

- Setting clear boundaries with others

- Dangers of impulsivity

- Staying dedicated to God

- Navigating complicated relationships with girls

- God's divine plan

- Trusting relationships

Leader Notes

_____

_____

_____

_____

_____

_____

_____

_____

_____

_____

Discussion

- How can setting clear boundaries and expectations impact relationships?

- What expectations does God place on us?

- What are the hallmarks of establishing trust in relationships?

- What does it mean to be impulsive?

- Can you name your God-given talents or gifts that make you different from other people?

Game Suggestion

Stomp the Yard

Lesson 9
REVIEW

Bible Personality
Review

Scripture
Review

Theme
Character

Potential Key Points
Open

Discussion
Open

Game Suggestion
Open

Sixty-Second Reflection Activity

Write the memory Scripture in your own words. What does this Scripture mean to you?

I praise you because I am fearfully and wonderfully made; your works are wonderful, I know that full well. – Psalms 139:14

_____

_____

_____

_____

_____

_____

_____

_____

_____

_____

_____

Lesson 10

Moses

Bible Personality
Moses

Scripture
Each group member reads a portion of Scripture pertaining to tonight's lesson.

Topic
Prayer: The act or practice of praying to God or a god. [1]

Theme
Discipleship

Scripture Reading
Exodus 33:1-17

Scripture Summary

God had an incredible relationship with Moses. They talked often and God gave Moses an incredible assignment. Moses was instructed by God to lead His people out of slavery in Egypt into a new land flowing with milk and honey. The land was occupied by other people, but God was so merciful that he informed Moses he would send an angel ahead of them to remove the people from the land.

In His mercy, God also recognized that His people were hard-headed and rebellious. He knew that if He continued to travel with them, they would continue to disrespect Him. The people's rebellious behavior would result in God's judgment and their destruction, so God decided the best way to protect them was to have them continue without Him.

God's people were sad when they heard He didn't want to travel with them. Being in a position between God and His people was challenging, so Moses spent a lot of time in prayer. He had a place outside of camp to commune with God. The place was called the Tent of Meeting. God met Moses at the Tent of Meeting, and they spent time together there. Everyone outside of the tent knew when the presence of the Lord arrived because something miraculous happened. A cloud of a pillar hovered over the tent when Moses met with God. Moses's assistant Joshua also spent time with Moses in the tent.

While in prayer, Moses asked the Lord for His plans for himself and the people. God spoke with him openly, like a friend.

He shared He would indeed travel with the people, and that everything would be fine for Moses.

Moses loved God, and he did not want to go anywhere without Him. Moses told God it was important to both him and the people for God to accompany them to the Promised Land. God responded favorably to Moses. He explained that because He cherished His relationship with Moses and knew him by name, He would do what Moses asked.

Key Points

Moses loved God and God loved Moses. They had a close friendship. Their relationship continued to grow over time and as Moses sought after God, God showed up for Moses.

Moses prayed. He asked questions of God. He sought God's plan for his life. Moses knew he needed God, and God responded. He showed love, mercy, and compassion for Moses and the people he was assigned to help.

Possible Talking Points

- Power of prayer

- Petition

- God's Sovereignty

- Dedication

- Modeling for others

- Personal Relationship with God

Leader Notes

_____

_____

_____

_____

_____

_____

_____

_____

_____

_____

Discussion

- Why do people pray?

- Why did Moses pray about God's presence staying with the people?

- How can you develop a life of prayer? How can your prayer life impact others?

- Based on the passage, is prayer a one-sided conversation?

- Why do you think people do not pursue a life of prayer?

Game Suggestion

Follow the Leader

Sixty-Second
Reflection Question

Moses had a life of prayer. He regularly communed with God. He was not afraid to pray to God for what he wanted. How can prayer help or hinder you?

_____

_____

_____

_____

_____

_____

_____

_____

_____

_____

_____

_____

Lesson 11
Daniel

Bible Personality
Daniel

Scripture
Each group member reads a portion of scripture pertaining to tonight's lesson.

Topic
Praise: An expression of approval: Commendation. [1]
Worship: To honor or show reverence for as a divine being or supernatural power. [2]

Theme
Discipleship

Scripture Reading
Daniel 1:1-17

Scripture Summary

The beautiful Jerusalem was under siege by King Nebuchadnezzar of Babylon. He even captured some of the Israelite nobles to go through several years of training for service in his palace.

Daniel was identified as a young man suitable for training. They changed his name and gave him royal clothing. The king also provided him with wine and meat from the palace, but the Israelites had their own special diet as an act of worship to God. Daniel insisted on remaining loyal to God, so he refused the king's food.

Daniel asked the king's head servant to give him only vegetables and water, but the servant feared the king would get angry if Daniel and his friends looked weak. Daniel was a young man of conviction, so he negotiated a plan with the king's staff. Daniel and his friends would eat the meals allowed by their faith for ten days and then go through tests to judge how they looked compared to the men who ate the king's meals.

Daniel knew God would bless his faithfulness. At the end of the test, Daniel and his friends looked healthier and better nourished than the others. He passed the test and was allowed to keep his special diet. God also granted Daniel the ability to learn faster and even interpret visions and dreams.

Key Points

Daniel was exiled to another country. He found himself at odds with the customs and practices of his new homeland. He was raised and taught to follow God, but in his new home the people and culture were different. Daniel had to make some tough decisions really quickly. How could he continue to serve God and disobey the leaders in his new environment? He knew he couldn't. Daniel decided to remain faithful and worship God despite what anyone else said.

Possible Talking Points

- Difficult Choices

- Culture clashes

- Conviction

- Belief Systems

- Worship Practices

- God's provision and favor

- Faith

Leader Notes

_____
_____
_____
_____
_____
_____
_____
_____
_____
_____
_____
_____

Discussion

- Would you rather play second string on a winning team or first string on a losing team?

- What makes you unique?

- What are the difficult aspects of being a leader?

- Explain the benefits of determination.

- What are you determined to do today? This month? This year? How can you make it happen?

- How can you praise God with your actions?

Game Suggestion

Stay Afloat

Sixty-Second Reflection Question

Daniel worshipped and honored God with his mind and body. He decided to make worship a part of his daily life, even when others did not want him to. Why do you think Daniel thought worshipping God was so important? In what ways can you praise and worship God in your daily life?

_____

_____

_____

_____

_____

_____

_____

_____

_____

_____

Lesson 12

REVIEW

Bible Personality
Review

Scripture
Review

Theme
Discipleship

Potential Key Points
Open

Discussion
Open

Game Suggestion
Group Party

Sixty-Second Reflection Activity

Write memory Scripture in your own words. What does this Scripture mean to you?

A new command I give you: Love one another. As I have loved you, so you must love one another. – John 13:34

_____

_____

_____

_____

_____

_____

_____

_____

_____

_____

Farewell

As the rain and the snow come down from heaven, and do not return to it without watering the earth and making it bud and flourish so that it yields seed for the sower and bread for the eater, so is my word that goes out from my mouth: it will not return to me empty, but will accomplish what I desire and achieve the purpose for which I sent it. – Isaiah 55:10-11

You did it! I am so proud of you and all the work you put in to organize, structure, teach, and disciple your Strong Roots group. In all groups, there are clear wins and some losses. May you celebrate every win and hold them close to your heart.

I am certain you and the Strong Roots group accomplished so much. It is my sincerest hope that, through this group, your students have learned more about God, the Bible, and themselves. Always know that the growth and spirituality you fostered by sharing the Word of God can never be erased.

God bless you and may His light shine through you always.

Warmly,

Bobi

STRONG
ROOTS

NOTES

NOTES

NOTES

NOTES

NOTES

Prayer to Start a Relationship with God

You can use this prayer as an example for your own prayer.

See Romans 10:9–10 for more about this relationship.

Dear God, I believe You are Lord. I acknowledge my sins before You now and ask I that You will forgive them. I turn away from my sins and turn my life into Your hands. I acknowledge You as Lord and confess that Jesus Christ is Your Son, who died on the cross, and You raised Him from the dead. Come into my heart. Lead and guide me always. I receive You by faith.

In Jesus's name.

Amen.

Acknowledgements

To my God,

Thank you. All the glory and honor belong to You. Great is thy faithfulness.

To my family,

Thank you for your love and patience.

To the FIGS and CIA Group Members,

Thank you for pushing me toward the more.

About the Author

Bobi Gentry Goodwin is a native of San Francisco. The Bay Area was where she first discovered her love for people and their stories. She has held a passion for writing since early childhood. As a clinical social worker, her mission field is working with women and children. She is a wife and mother of two and an avid member of her local church. Bobi is a licensed minister, Bible study leader, and host of the Finding Forever Podcast. Her writing has been featured in *Chicken Soup for the Soul.* She is also a member of Delta Sigma Theta Sorority, Inc. Goodwin currently resides with her family in sunny California.

Also by Bobi Gentry Goodwin

Visit her at <u>www.bobigentrygoodwin.com</u>

Revelation by Bobi Gentry Goodwin

She Writes Press

$16.95, 978-1-63152-606-0

The lives of social worker Angela Lovelace and five-year-old boy Trevion are changed forever when they meet at the scene of his mother's death. While conducting her investigation, she discovers her father's picture at the site. Angela is a well-trained worker and never had a sleepless night until now as she grapples with this grim discovery. Fear, anxiety, and family secrets unfold as she sets out to uncover the truth.

Endnotes

1. Merriam-Webster.com Dictionary, s.v. "vision," accessed March 12, 2023, https://www.merriam-webster.com/dictionary/vision.

2. Merriam-Webster.com Dictionary, s.v. "vice," accessed March 12, 2023, https://www.merriam-webster.com/dictionary/vice.

3. Merriam-Webster.com Dictionary, s.v. "courage," accessed March 12, 2023, https://www.merriam-webster.com/dictionary/courage.

4. Merriam-Webster.com Dictionary, s.v. "confidence," accessed March 12, 2023, https://www.merriam-webster.com/dictionary/confidence.

5. Merriam-Webster.com Dictionary, s.v. "conviction," accessed April 7, 2023, https://www.merriam-webster.com/dictionary/conviction.

6. Merriam-Webster.com Dictionary, s.v. "gift," accessed March 12, 2023, https://www.merriam-webster.com/dictionary/gift.

7. Merriam-Webster.com Dictionary, s.v. "prayer," accessed March 12, 2023, https://www.merriam-webster.com/dictionary/prayer.

8. Merriam-Webster.com Dictionary, s.v. "praise," accessed March 12, 2023, https://www.merriam-webster.com/dictionary/praise.

9. Merriam-Webster.com Dictionary, s.v. "worship," accessed March 12, 2023, https://www.merriam-webster.com/dictionary/worship.